THE FIRST BOOK OF
THE CLIFF DWELLERS

Balcony House, a cliff dwelling built into a cave at the edge of a cliff in Mesa Verde, Colorado. (National Park Service)

THE FIRST BOOK OF
THE CLIFF DWELLERS

by
Rebecca B. Marcus

Illustrated with photographs

Drawings by
Julio Granda

Franklin Watts, Inc.
575 Lexington Avenue
New York, N.Y. 10022

The author wishes to thank Mr. Richard M. Howard, Supervisory Archaeologist at Mesa Verde National Park, Colorado, for his critical reading of the manuscript. The author also thanks the men and women of the National Park Service for their valuable assistance in obtaining photographs used in this book.

To David and Jonathan, who can hardly wait to become old enough to see the Cliff Dwellings for themselves.

CONTENTS

Abandoned "apartment house" cliff dwelling in southwest Colorado (National Park Service)

OUT OF THE PAST

A big, terraced, four-story apartment house stands deserted in a cave high in a canyon wall in southwestern Colorado. The house was built about 750 years ago. No iron or other kind of metal tool was used in its construction, for its builders knew nothing about the use of metals. The apartment house was abandoned by the year 1300. As in a ghost town the house crumbled, and its ruins blended in with the color of the rock of the cave.

1

One of the small cliff dwellings that dot the face of Navajo Canyon (National Park Service)

A few other large, deserted apartment houses and many clusters of small, crumbling dwellings dotted the faces of the canyon cliffs. No one was known to have explored any of these ruins for hundreds of years. The Ute Indians living in the Mancos River valley nearby avoided the ghostly houses. They believed that the ruins were haunted by the spirits of the dead.

North rim of Mesa Verde towering above the valley (National Park Service)

The white men who first came into southwestern Colorado were Spaniards looking for gold and silver. Later, white settlers became miners, farmers, and cattle ranchers. They paid little heed to rumors of ancient cliff dwellings in the caves of the canyons near the Mancos River. But the white men could not help noticing a flat-topped mountain rising in steep cliffs above the river valley. Because the mountain looked like a

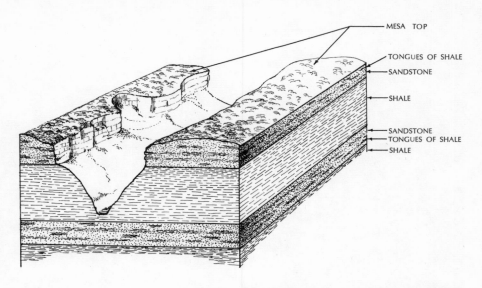

MESA TOP

TONGUES OF SHALE
SANDSTONE

SHALE

SANDSTONE
TONGUES OF SHALE
SHALE

Composition of the rock of Mesa Verde

great green-topped tableland, the Spaniards called it *Mesa Verde*, the Spanish words for "Green Table."

The rock of Mesa Verde and of the region around it was formed under the sea about a hundred million years ago. This was the time in the earth's history called the Cretaceous Period. For millions of years, streams continued to wear down the land, so that most of the region now stands more than 6,000 feet above sea level. One great block standing above the rest of the land slopes from the north toward the southeast. It towers 2,000 feet above the plain at the north, and 1,300 feet at the southeast. Much of its top is covered with juniper and piñon pine trees. This block is the one called Mesa Verde.

4

Fingers of land in Mesa Verde as they appear viewed from the air
(National Park Service)

The rock composing it is mostly in layers of sandstone of different hardness. Bands of still harder shale are found between some of the sandstone layers. Over many thousands of years, streams flowing into the Mancos River have cut a number of long canyons into the rock. Narrow fingers of land have been left extending out of the main block of the mountain. Where the rock was exposed in the walls of the mesa fingers, water seeped in between the layers. Repeated freezing of this water in winter and thawing in spring weakened the rock and caused it to crack. Gradually, the cracked rock broke away from the wall, leaving a cave with an overhanging roof and a floor of hard rock.

5

Today, as one rides westward from Durango, Colorado, the green tableland, Mesa Verde, looms up on the left almost straight above the valley. No caves can be seen from the road. Nor can a visitor there guess that, clinging to the walls of its many canyons, are the remains of ancient cliff dwellings and of the Cliff Dwellers — the people who lived in them.

A sheer wall of rock towering above a valley at Mesa Verde (National Park Service)

DISCOVERY OF THE CLIFF DWELLINGS

In 1874, the United States Government sent a surveying party into southwestern Colorado. William H. Jackson, a famous photographer of that time, was a member of the party. While the party was stationed in the Mancos River valley, Jackson heard rumors from local mining prospectors of old Indian ruins in the cliffs of Mesa Verde. He himself thought the stories of cliff dwellings sounded improbable, but one of the prospectors, John Moss, offered to act as his guide to the ruins. So Jackson decided to investigate.

Jackson's photograph of Two-Story Cliff House, taken in 1874 (U.S. Department of the Interior)

Sure enough, Moss led Jackson to a ruined two-storied stone dwelling built into a small cave in the face of a cliff. Jackson gave the name "Two-Story Cliff House" to this dwelling. He photographed it and several other small ones that he found, and sent copies of the photographs together with a report to Washington.

The next year a government geologist, William H. Holmes, discovered other small ruins in Mesa Verde. He, too, sent a report of his find to Washington. The reports of Jackson and Holmes were filed, but no further investigation of the ruins was made at that time.

The Wetherill brothers. The curved black line is a crack in the glass-plate negative. Left to right: Al, Win, Richard, Clayton, and John (U.S. Department of the Interior)

As it turned out, the greatest discovery in Mesa Verde was made, not by government men, but by two cowboys, Richard Wetherill and his brother-in-law Charles Mason.

The Wetherill family lived on a ranch in the Mancos River valley. The three brothers, Alfred, Richard, and John, often ran cattle in the canyons that cut into Mesa Verde. Sometimes they explored small cliff dwellings that they found in the canyon walls.

One day an Indian told them about a ruined cliff dwelling in a big cave in one of the Mesa Verde canyons. According to the Indian's description, this cliff dwelling was tremen-

9

Cliff Palace a few months after it was discovered. The ruin had not yet been repaired. (Smithsonian Office of Anthropology, Bureau of American Ethnology)

dous. The Wetherills found the story hard to believe, but they did not forget it.

It was snowing on December 18, 1888. Richard Wetherill and Charles Mason were rounding up stray cattle in the canyons of Mesa Verde. They followed the trail of the cattle to the mesa top, and along the tree-covered tableland. The trail led them near the edge of the mesa, to a place where the growth of juniper and piñon pines thinned out.

The cowboys looked across the canyon and saw an amazing sight in the cliff opposite them. High in the wall was a very large cave with an overhanging roof that protected it com-

10

pletely from the snow. A great cliff dwelling filled the cave. This, they thought, must be the tremendous cliff dwelling the Indian had described.

The two men rode along the mesa top until they were just above the dwelling. Then they noticed a faint trail leading down to the cave, and followed it.

Here is Charles Mason's own account of their first entrance into the ruins:

"We rode around the head of the canyon and found a way down over the cliffs to the level of the buildings. We spent several hours going from room to room and picked up several articles of interest."

The cowboys called the dwelling "Cliff Palace" because of its great size, but no one knows for certain which of them first thought of the name. Later that day, Richard discovered another smaller dwelling about three miles from Cliff Palace. This dwelling has since been called Spruce Tree House.

Greatly excited, Wetherill and Mason rode back to the ranch and reported their discovery. Their story gripped the interest of Wetherill's brother, John. With three friends he followed the trail to Cliff Palace to see for himself. These four men, too, were struck by the great size of the dwelling. They explored the cave at greater length than had Richard Wetherill and Charles Mason. In fact, John stayed in the cave for a whole month and made a detailed examination of it.

As news of the discovery of Cliff Palace and Spruce Tree House spread, many questions arose about the dwellings. Who had built them? What were the people like, how had they lived, why had they abandoned their homes? The answers to

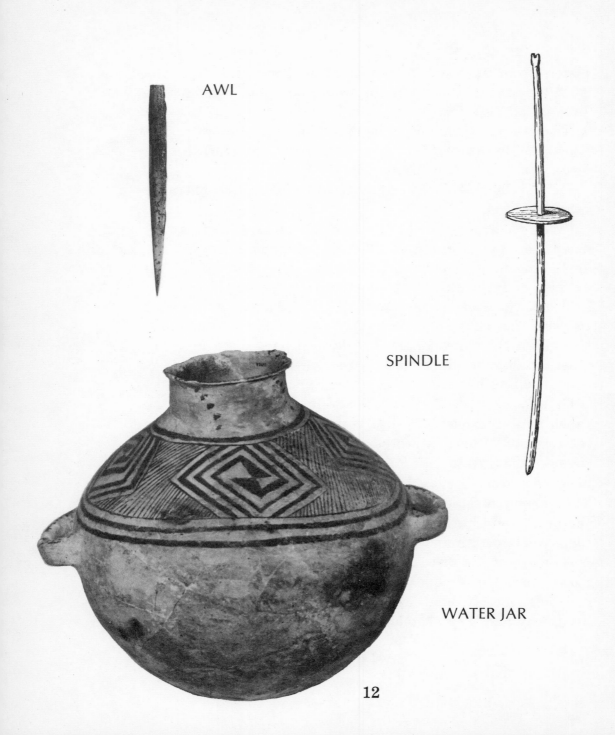

AWL

SPINDLE

WATER JAR

12

these questions had to wait until careful study was made of the ruins and of the articles found in them. But one thing was certain — the Cliff Dwellers had been Indians. Articles found in the dwellings resembled those used by many Pueblo Indian tribes still living in the nearby river valleys.

JUG

DIPPER

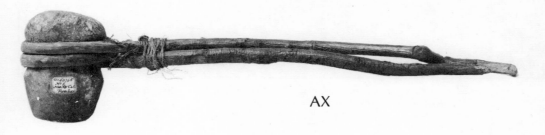

AX

Some of the articles found in cliff dwellings
(National Park Service)
(Smithsonian Office of Anthropology, Bureau of American Ethnology)

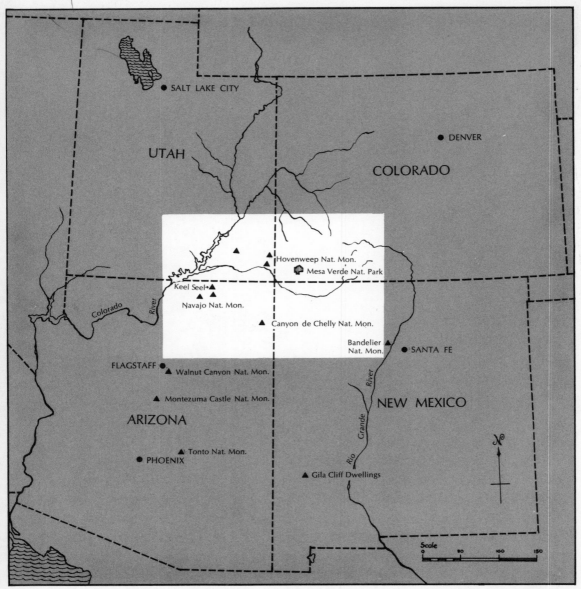

Map giving location of cliff dwellings. The white center area includes the Four Corners

Keet Seel in the Navajo National Monument in Arizona. This is the second largest cliff dwelling known. (National Park Service)

People came from near and far — from as far away as Sweden — to see the remarkable cliff dwellings. Among them were scientists, but there were also those who came out of curiosity. Visitors dug around for souvenirs and removed artifacts — pottery, baskets, tools, and various other articles. Some of the artifacts went into the visitors' homes, but many of them were sold to museums and collectors for profit.

Betatakin Cliff Dwelling in the Navajo National Monument. The rock of the canyon serves as a wall in some of these dwellings. (National Park Service)

In 1906, eighteen years after the large cliff dwellings were discovered, the United States Government decided to take a hand in preserving the ruins. Mesa Verde was declared a national park, and a park superintendent was appointed. Rangers and archaeologists (scientists who study the relics left by ancient man) in the government service went about clearing the rubble. They repaired some of the walls to make the park safe for visitors. Today, Mesa Verde is one of the chief attractions for visitors to the Southwest.

16

The "White House," built into a cave at Canyon de Chelly National Monument (National Park Service)

The discovery of the Mesa Verde cliff dwellings spurred the search for others in the Southwest. The search resulted in the discovery of a number of other cliff dwellings. Many of them are in the "Four Corners" region, where Utah, Colorado, Arizona, and New Mexico meet. The second largest, next to Cliff Palace, is Keet Seel, in northeastern Arizona in the Navajo National Monument. Another very large one is also in northeast Arizona, in the Canyon de Chelly (pronounced Canyon de Shay) on the Navajo Indian reservation. The

17

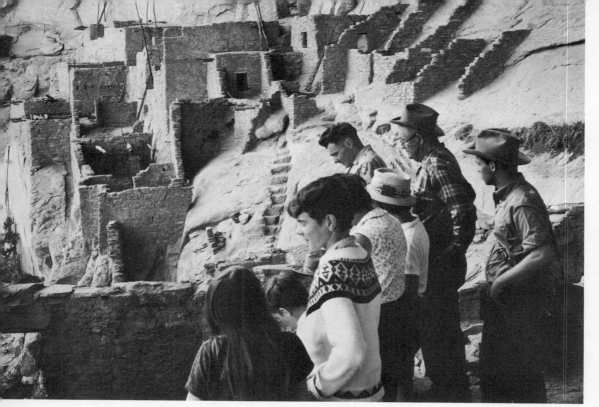

A National Park Service ranger guides a group of visitors through a cliff dwelling in the Canyon de Chelly National Monument. (National Park Service)

map on page 14 shows the Four Corners, and the location of most of the known cliff dwellings.

The Mesa Verde cliff dwellings are the most spectacular ever found. And, perhaps because they were the first to be found, they have been studied by more scientists than any of the others. For the most part, this book will deal with the Mesa Verde Cliff Dwellers, for scientists are quite sure that the life of the other Cliff Dwellers was very much like that of the inhabitants of Mesa Verde.

18

DATING THE CLIFF DWELLINGS –
TREE-RING DATING

None of the Indians living at the time the cliff dwellings were discovered knew anything about the people who had inhabited them. No songs or stories remained about Cliff Dwellers. Therefore archaeologists assumed the cliff dwellings must probably be very old. But just *how* old?

At first no one could tell. But in the early 1900's a way was found to pinpoint almost exactly the age of the cliff dwellings and of other old structures as well. The discoverer of the method was Dr. Andrew E. Douglass of the University of Arizona. It is called tree-ring dating, or *dendrochronology*, a word that stems from two Greek words meaning "tree" and

19

"time." Tree-ring dating can be used if there are any wooden beams or poles in a structure, or sometimes if charcoal is found in a dwelling.

This is how tree-ring dating works:

Underneath the outer bark of a tree is the growth layer of the tree trunk or of a branch. This layer is called the *cambium*. The cambium surrounds the actual wood of the tree. Each year, during spring and summer, the cambium grows new wood. The new wood is fairly soft. After the growing season, this soft new wood hardens and forms a distinct ring around the wood grown during the previous year. The ring is always wider during a year when growing conditions are good than it is during a year when less favorable conditions prevail.

Each ring is called an *annual ring*. The trunk and branches of a tree increase in diameter by the addition of annual rings. Since a new ring is formed each year, the number of annual rings shows the age of a tree. By cutting across a log, or boring out a core through a living tree, and then counting the annual rings, a person can tell the tree's age. He can also tell something about what the weather conditions were during the time a particular ring was growing.

Dr. Douglass was an astronomer. He was trying to find a connection between sunspots and the weather on our earth. His research led him to study the annual rings of trees to learn about the earth's weather conditions. But soon Douglass discovered that he needed to know exactly which years certain annual rings were formed. This was easy enough to find out in a tree that had just been cut. It was only necessary to

BARK

CAMBIUM

ANNUAL RING

175 Years

12 Years

Cross-section of a log. The tree was 187 years old when cut. (Weyer-haeuser Company)

A core being bored out of a tree (Weyerhaeuser Company)

count the years backward from the outermost ring. But it became a different matter indeed when he did not know which year a tree had been cut down. To find out more precisely, he devised an ingenious scheme.

First, Douglass made a diagram of the annual rings of a newly cut tree. Such a diagram is called a *profile*. He looked for a distinctive pattern made by the annual rings. For example, he may have noticed that beginning 20 years earlier and counting inward, there were five unusually narrow growth rings. Then there might be three wider rings, and, next to these, two quite wide ones. Douglass would take this pattern to mean that the growing season 20 years earlier marked the end of a five-year dry spell. Then, before the dry spell, there had been three years of normal rainfall; and, before those three years, a two-year rainy spell.

Next, Douglass made a profile of the annual rings of a log cut some years earlier. He did not have to know the date the log was cut. Instead, he looked for a distinctive pattern in its annual rings that matched a pattern in the rings he had already dated. When he found two patterns that matched, he was able to proceed with his calculations. From the first log he had learned the dates when these rings were formed. By counting the annual rings from the pattern in the second, older one, he would be able to date the log.

Thus, by working backward step by step, log by log, Douglass could find out the age of almost any log. He spent months in Indian villages in the southwestern United States looking for old beams that had been cut with stone axes. He reasoned that such beams had probably been salvaged from ancient dwellings for present use by the Indians living in the villages. And with the aid of archaeologists, he also studied sections of beams found in old Indian ruins.

As a result of all this work, Douglass was able to draw up a chart of annual tree rings dating from the present day back to A.D. 11 This same chart still serves as a calendar for the dating of wood in the Southwest.

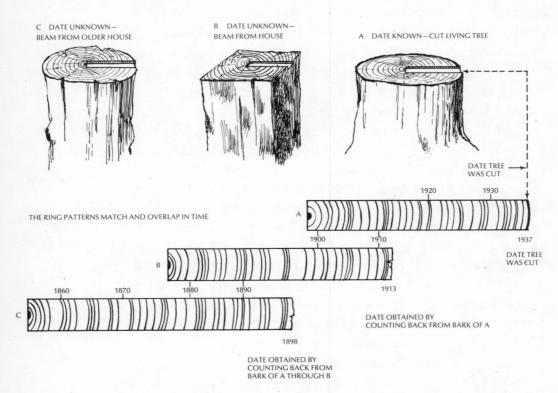

C   DATE UNKNOWN—
BEAM FROM OLDER HOUSE

B   DATE UNKNOWN—
BEAM FROM HOUSE

A   DATE KNOWN—CUT LIVING TREE

DATE TREE
WAS CUT

1920   1930

THE RING PATTERNS MATCH AND OVERLAP IN TIME

A

1900   1910   1937

DATE TREE
WAS CUT

B

1860   1870   1880   1890   1913

C

DATE OBTAINED BY
COUNTING BACK FROM BARK OF A

1898

DATE OBTAINED BY
COUNTING BACK FROM
BARK OF A THROUGH B

Method of tree-ring dating (Laboratory of Tree-ring Research. After Stallings)

By using Douglass' tree-ring dating calendar, scientists were able to learn that the cliff dwellings were built beginning about the year 1200 — and abandoned by 1300. Most of the cliff dwellings elsewhere were also abandoned by that time, or shortly thereafter.

24

CLIFF DWELLER VILLAGES

Most of the Cliff Dwellers lived in small villages consisting of one dwelling sufficient for only a few dozen people. The walls of the canyons in Mesa Verde are dotted with hundreds of these small cliff dwellings set in shallow caves. Probably there were so many small villages because there were far more small caves than large ones.

The dwellings in the small villages were mostly one story high, and built of sandstone blocks held together by clay masonry. Small stones were embedded in the clay for added strength. The roofs were made of wooden beams and branches plastered over with clay. Some of the dwellings had low, narrow doors, barely big enough for an adult to enter. Many had no door at all, only an opening in the roof. A person had to climb a ladder to the roof and then down another ladder into the dwelling.

Small stones embedded in clay masonry added strength to walls of cliff dwellings. (National Park Service)

Turkey bones found in the ruins show that the Cliff Dwellers raised turkeys; likewise, the bones of deer and mountain sheep reveal that the people hunted those animals for food. But the many dried ears of corn, and bean and squash seeds found in the caves and dwellings show that the Cliff Dwellers were chiefly farmers. Yet there could be no fields in the caves or anywhere in the canyon walls in which to grow crops. The top of the mesa itself afforded the only land suitable for cultivation.

It seemed strange to the early explorers of Mesa Verde that the people farmed their crops on the mesa top yet lived in the cliff walls. Bit by bit, however, scientists pieced together information that told them the probable reason for this. A village built high in a cliff was reasonably safe from enemy attack. An invader had to climb down the cliff from the mesa top by a narrow trail or by means of ropes, ladders, or toeholds in the rock. The defenders of the village could thus easily repel an enemy attack.

This cliff dwelling built in the cliff wall was reasonably safe from attack.

CLIFF PALACE – THE "BIG TOWN"

Cliff Palace and the other large settlements were big towns. To us, living in the twentieth century, they may seem small, but to people living in tiny villages they must have seemed huge. The three- and four-story houses must have looked very tall to people who lived in low one-story buildings.

The big towns were centers of trade and of important religious ceremonies. The Cliff Dwellers in small villages probably looked forward to the excitement of a visit to the big town. There they could trade goods, gamble, learn the latest styles, gossip, and exchange ideas.

28

Cliff Palace as it appears today (National Park Service)

Cliff Palace was not really a palace in which a king, a prince, or a rich family lived. Rather, it was a large structure with many rooms, housing about 200 people. Like the houses in the small villages, it was built of sandstone blocks cemented together with clay into which were stuck small stones. It was set in a crescent-shaped cave 325 feet across the front end. The cave's greatest depth from the back to the edge of the cliff was about 100 feet. The dwelling, built like a terraced apartment house, was fitted into the sheltering cave. The many rooms rose from the front in at least eight levels up from the sloping floor of the cave. A long row of small storage rooms was built on a ledge at the back of the cave.

The walls of the buildings, as in most of the other cliff dwellings, are *plumb* — that is, exactly vertical. They were built at right angles to each other and still stand that way. There is also a tall round tower in Cliff Palace. The walls of this tower are almost perfectly circular.

A person who views Cliff Palace today cannot help but marvel at the great skill shown by its builders. They had nothing but simple stone tools. They could not quarry sandstone blocks with these tools, nor had they any means of carrying very large boulders. They had to use such blocks as they could find and carry into the cave. In addition, they had to chip and flake the rock into the size and shape needed for the building.

The dwelling was divided into rooms about eight by six feet in size. Entrance into the rooms was through a small doorway or through an opening in the roof. The rooms on a level above the floor of the cave were reached by a ladder from the cave floor or from the roof of the building on the level below them.

Plumb walls and round tower at Cliff Palace (National Park Service)

Geometric designs decorating the walls of a room in a cliff dwelling (National Park Service)

Most of the rooms had niches in them for storing food, clothing, and other materials. Wooden pegs on which to hang things were set into the walls of some rooms. The walls were plastered with clay slapped on and smoothed with the hands. Handprints have been found dried into the clay, indicating the method of applying the plaster.

Many walls were decorated with red, yellow, green, white, black, or brown geometric designs. Some walls had figures of birds or other small animals. An unusual decoration was found above the door of one of the rooms. It shows a row of nine left hands, all alike, painted in red. It looks as if the artist placed her left hand on the wall, traced its outline with her right hand, and then filled in the outline.

Each family had several rooms, some for sleeping and some for storage. As in some Indian villages today, the family slept on the floor with mats or blankets under them. There is evidence to show that fires were built in the sleeping rooms, but were probably used only in bad weather. Ventilation was so poor, however, that when a fire was made the room soon became uncomfortably smoky.

Fires were generally built outside the dwelling, in shallow pits dug into the front part of the cave floor. The front of the cave was one big courtyard. Much of the life of the people was spent there and on the flat roofs of the terraced houses. Here the family cooked and ate its meals, ground corn, wove cloth, played with the children, and carried on its other activities. Trash was simply thrown out of the cave, or piled in back behind the dwelling.

THE KIVA, OR CEREMONIAL ROOM

Dug into the floor of the cave were a number of round underground rooms with walls about six feet high. These rooms resembled the underground rooms found in many Pueblo Indian settlements today. The Hopi Indians, one of the Pueblo tribes, call these rooms *kivas*. The kivas are used mainly as religious ceremonial rooms. Archaeologists therefore reasoned that those in Cliff Palace and in other cliff dwellings were used for the same purpose. And, as among the Hopis, each clan had its own kiva. In the cave in which Cliff Palace stands, twenty-three kivas have been found.

Interior of a kiva. A flat roof once covered the entire structure. (Smithsonian Office of Anthropology, Bureau of American Ethnology)

The kivas were all built according to the same pattern. The floor was of packed earth. Masonry pillars, usually six in number, supported a roof made of layers of logs covered over with earth. An opening was left in the roof which served both as a means of entrance into the kiva and for smoke to escape. A shelf for storage was set all around the walls.

An opening at one point in the base of the wall led to a small tunnel. The tunnel was bent to form an L-shaped air

35

shaft that opened into the floor of the cave. The floor of the structure had a shallow fire pit hollowed out a few feet from the tunnel entrance. A slab of sandstone was set upright between the tunnel opening and the fire pit. The slab acted as a deflector that prevented air from blowing directly on the fire and prevented drafts.

Each kiva also had a small hole in the center of the floor. Present-day Hopis call this hole a *sipapu*. According to them, it is the entrance to the underworld in which the spirits of the gods live.

From the outside, only the top of the ventilating shaft and the entrance, with the ladder extending through the opening, could be seen. The flat roof blended in with the floor of the cave and became part of the courtyard.

In addition to serving as religious ceremonial rooms, the kivas served as the men's clubrooms and workshops. Women and girls were rarely permitted to enter. There the men wove blankets, made sandals and rope from yucca fiber, and performed other work that could be done indoors. Stories were told, legends recounted, and songs and chants were taught the older boys.

The kivas were the most comfortable structures in the settlement. They had good ventilation and warm fires. Fresh air entered a kiva through the air shaft and tunnel; smoke from the fire escaped through the opening in the roof; and the deflector kept out drafts. It is therefore not surprising that the men sometimes preferred to sleep in the kiva instead of in the badly ventilated rooms of the cliff dwelling itself.

36

WATER FOR THE BIG TOWNS

The Cliff Dwellers lived in a semi-arid region where it seldom rained except in the spring and late summer. Nor were there any streams on the mesa. The people, therefore, had to depend mainly on natural springs for their water supply.

In Cliff Palace most of the water was brought in from small springs that came out at the base of the cliff. The women and girls filled jars with water that collected in pools fed by these springs. Then they balanced the jars on doughnut-shaped head pads and carried them on their heads back to the dwelling. One of the finest springs used by the Cliff Palace people was across the canyon, half a mile away by trail. This was a considerable distance to carry a jar of water, but the water was clear, good-tasting, and its flow was dependable.

Rests for pottery jars (Smithsonian Office of Anthropology, Bureau of American Ethnology)

During the rainy season, the women set out jars to catch the rain water. The filled jars were then stored in the family rooms for use during the dry season. In the rainy season, too, water may have been made to collect in artificial pools along the slope below Cliff Palace. Archaeologists have found low walls that appear to have been a series of dams along the slope. These dams would have provided catch basins for rain water.

Spruce Tree House was probably also considered a big town. As in Cliff Palace, the dwelling was built in terraces rising toward the back of the cave. But Spruce Tree House had one advantage over Cliff Palace. An excellent spring very near the cave gave a dependable supply of good water. The spring is still flowing today.

A third town, Balcony House, had a spring of good drinking water in the rear of the cave itself. Thus it was not necessary for the women to carry water except from the back of the cave into the courtyard and dwelling.

Spruce Tree House. At left, a ladder leads down into a kiva. (National Park Service)

BALCONY HOUSE

Besides having a spring right in the cave, the people who lived in Balcony House had better protection against enemies than the other Cliff Dwellers. Their dwelling was built in a cave that was almost impossible to invade. Only a narrow ledge about 400 feet long separated the front of the cave from a sheer 30-foot drop down to the slope of the canyon. One end of this ledge came right up against the cliff. The other end came to a narrow cleft in the rock through which the top could be reached.

40

Balcony House. Visitors must climb a 30-foot ladder to enter the ruin.
(National Park Service)

The Cliff Dwellers of Balcony House walled up this cleft
to a height of about 15 feet, but left a narrow tunnel in the
base of the wall. A person had to crawl on his hands and
knees to enter the cliff dwelling from the mesa above. Thus a
few defenders could stand at the mouth of the tunnel and pick
off any attackers one by one as they tried to enter the cave.

Balcony and parapet at Balcony House (National Park Service)

Balcony House rose two stories from the floor of the cave to its overhanging roof. It was the best-constructed dwelling found in Mesa Verde. It was built well into the cave, leaving a courtyard in front for family and community activities, and for its two kivas. A low wall, or parapet, was built along the cliff edge of the courtyard. Doubtless this was to prevent children — and adults as well — from falling over the cliff.

Narrow walks and balconies extended outside the house under the doorways of the upper rooms, and led from one room to the next. The cliff dwelling is called Balcony House because of these balconies.

It was impossible to walk upright through the doorway of a room in Balcony House. Most of the doors were only about 16 inches wide and 24 inches high, with doorsills rising two or three feet from the floor. A person had to climb over the sill and duck his head through the doorway.

Like the other Cliff Dwellers, Balcony House Indians were farmers. Daily, during the growing season, the men climbed through the tunnel to the mesa top. There they cultivated the fields and later harvested the crop. The men also hunted game and the women cured the skins of the animals to make clothing and blankets.

The spring in the cave supplied the people with water for their daily needs, but it could not supply water for the crops. Beginning with the year 1273, the harvest was poor. A long severe drought hit Mesa Verde and the land around it. The Indians of Balcony House were well protected against a living enemy, but they could not keep out an equally dangerous enemy — hunger. Probably for this reason, and perhaps for other unknown reasons as well, Balcony House was abandoned. No charred wood, charcoal, or wooden beams show a date later than 1282. Soon after that, the last of its dwellers had left Balcony House.

Cliff Palace, Spruce Tree House, and Balcony House are not the only large cliff dwellings found in Mesa Verde National Park, but they are the best excavated. In 1958, work was begun to clear away the rubble of several cliff dwellings in Wetherill Mesa in the southwestern part of the park. The work was completed in 1963. The largest dwelling cleared, known as Long House, is the second largest in Mesa Verde, but smaller than Keet Seel, a cliff dwelling in Arizona.

An archaeologist climbing down a cliff to reach a small dwelling in Wetherill Mesa.

THE MYSTERIOUS SUN TEMPLE

On the top of the mesa, across the canyon from Cliff Palace, is a mysterious structure that has been given the name of Sun Temple. It shows no signs of ever being used as a dwelling. In fact, no one has discovered what its actual use was. Yet it became known as Sun Temple because some of its features hint that secret religious rituals were performed there.

Sun Temple is a D-shaped structure 121 feet long and 64 feet wide. It does not seem ever to have had a roof, and is open to the sky. It has an outer double wall about 8 to 10

Sun Temple, with double outer wall and doorless rooms (National Park Service)

feet high. Between the two parts of the wall are a number of small rooms. Nine of these rooms have no doors and can be entered only from the top. There are 25 rooms in all. In the center of the courtyard enclosed by the walls are two kivas, and a third is off to a side.

The entire building was built around the three kivas. This fact, plus the lack of a roof and the nine doorless rooms, has led archaeologists to think that the structure had some religious significance.

There are other buildings in Mesa Verde that may have been used only for religious purposes, but there is no way of knowing this for sure. One building, standing alone in a cave, may have been such a one. It, too, does not appear to have been used as a dwelling. Some of its walls are blackened by smoke, showing that fires were built inside it a great many times. For this reason, the building was given the name Fire Temple. Was it ever really a temple? No one knows, nor is anyone ever likely to find out.

This round tower in Wetherill Mesa was probably used for religious ceremonies.

PIECING TOGETHER A PUZZLE

The Cliff Dwellers, like people all over the world, had their good days and their bad days. They laughed and sang, were sad and cried, became angry and then calmed their anger. They scolded their children when necessary — sometimes when it was not necessary, too — and they gave praise when it was deserved. And, also like people everywhere, the adults taught their children the skills they would need in later life.

There were differences among individuals, too. Some were more artistic than others, some women were better house-keepers and cooks, some were fine pottery makers. Some men had a gift for telling stories, others composed songs and chants. There were particularly good hunters among them and especially industrious farmers, just as there were also poor hunters and lazy farmers.

Woven sandals found in Mesa Verde. (Smithsonian Office of Anthropology, Bureau of American Ethnology)

Bit by bit, like fitting pieces into a jigsaw puzzle, scientists have been able to piece together a picture of life in a cliff dwelling. To do this they have had to draw upon different fields of knowledge for information.

First, when archaeologists exposed the ruins, they found many household articles, pieces of clothing, long pointed sticks, stone knives and scrapers, bows and arrows, and other implements. The uses of many of these articles were obvious. A big watertight pottery jar probably was used for storing water. A tightly woven basket with a few dried kernels of corn caught in the bottom must have been used to store corn. A small piece of matting shaped like the sole of a foot, and with straps across it, could only have been a sandal. But there were other articles with which they were unfamiliar. They turned for help to historical records and to *ethnologists* (scientists who study the life and customs of people).

The records left by early Spanish explorers contain descriptions of the ways of life of the Pueblo Indians whom they found living in the region. These Indians, most likely descendants of the Cliff Dwellers, probably still retained many of the ancient customs. It became necessary, therefore, to examine the records of the Spaniards in order to learn the use of some of the finds. In this way, a picture of the life of the Cliff Dwellers began to emerge.

But there were pieces missing in the picture. What was their religion like? What were the activities in the kiva? How was the work of the community divided? Such questions and many more were unanswered.

In order to study the customs of the Indians of the Four Corners region, some ethnologists went to live in the Indian villages. The ethnologists often gained the friendship and confidence of the Indians. They learned the legends and songs of the modern Indians. Many of the songs and legends were so old they might possibly have been those of the Cliff Dwellers. Some ethnologists came to be so greatly trusted by the Indians that they were allowed to enter the kiva, and some were even admitted to the priesthood. Some were permitted

Modern Pueblo Indians, descendants of the Cliff Dwellers (U.S. Department of the Interior, Bureau of Indian Affairs)

to witness and partake in healing ceremonies rarely seen by outsiders.

Thus, the story of life in a cliff dwelling was unfolded. However, no one can ever be certain about all the ways of life of an ancient people who left no written records. For some of the customs of the Hopi, Zuñi, and other Pueblo Indians of the Southwest changed as they came into contact with white

51

men. Many of their implements, and their style of clothing, too, changed over the many years. Ethnologists admit that, in reconstructing the life of the Cliff Dwellers, they must make some guesses. But they think they have a good solid basis for making them.

It was hardly necessary to guess what the Cliff Dwellers looked like. When John Wetherill explored Cliff Palace he found, in the storage rooms at the back of the cave, fourteen mummified bodies. The bodies were wrapped in several layers of matting and cloth. An examination of the bodies and of those found elsewhere showed what the appearance of the people must have been like.

The Cliff Dwellers, for the most part, looked like modern Pueblo Indians. They were short to average in height, had long straight black hair, and high cheekbones. A fold of fat on the inner part of the eyelids near the nose made the eyes appear slanting. Scientists use the word "Mongoloid" in describing these features.

But the shape of the heads of the Cliff Dwellers differed in a marked way from the heads of other people with Mongoloid features. The back of the head of every mummy and every skull was flat. The flatness distorted the skull and made the face wider than those of other Indians.

Among the artifacts found in cliff dwellings were flat oblong boards two to three feet long, made of split branches tied together. Lacings attached to the sides could be tied to hold down anything placed on the flat board. A loop that appeared to be a carrying strap was fastened across one short side.

Cradle board found in Mesa Verde. The holes show where straps were fastened. (National Park Service)

Archaeologists figured out that these were cradleboards. Infants were tied onto these boards from the time they were born until they were about 15 months old. During those first 15 months of an infant's life its skull is soft enough to be shaped flat by a cradleboard. This, then, explained the distorted shape of the Cliff Dwellers' skulls.

Examination of the mummies and of skeletons found in cliff dwellings also showed that many of the people suffered from rheumatism and arthritis. Bad teeth were common. All of these evidences point to the fact that life, particularly in the winter when people with arthritis suffer most, was generally not easy for the Cliff Dwellers.

This board was found in Wetherill Mesa. The hole at one end shows it was probably part of a cradleboard.

LIFE IN A CLIFF DWELLING –
AUTUMN

Imagine life in a cliff dwelling in about the year 1270.

In the autumn the men and boys carried down many baskets
laden with ripe ears of corn, beans, and squash from the fields
on the mesa top. They had no animals to help them carry the
harvest, nor any other means of making the burden easier.
The work was slow, but the men and boys were cheerful, for
the harvest was plentiful.

September in Spruce Tree House (Diorama in Museum at Mesa Verde National Park)

The women and girls set out the cut crop on the rooftops to dry. They also gathered roots, berries, and fruits to dry and store for the winter. After the foods dried they were placed in baskets and jars and stored in niches in the rooms, or in small storage rooms. Piñon nuts, the seeds of the piñon pine, were gathered in large quantities. The little oval, cream-colored kernels of these nuts were a great favorite with the Cliff Dwellers.

56

Harvest dance of Zuñi Indians. Except for dress, the Cliff Dwellers' dance was probably much like this. (Santa Fe Railway)

Autumn was also the big hunting season. When the men brought in their kill, the women dried the extra meat and stored it. They tanned the animal skins and made clothing and blankets of the soft leather. They used bone awls to punch small holes in the leather so as to pass the bone needle through the skins easily. The thread was made of yucca fiber or of cotton string. The Cliff Dwellers did not grow cotton, but received it in trade with settlements to the south.

The men worked at making feather cloth which was mainly used for blankets. To do this they twisted turkey feathers in spirals around strands of yucca fiber. This made a fluffy yarn for weaving into warm cloth for the winter.

In late fall, just before winter set in, important religious ceremonies were held. At this time the older boys were invited to sleep in the kiva, away from their mothers and the other children. The boys were taught the chants and other parts of the religious ceremonies. During this period the men seldom left the kivas. Except for bringing them food, the women left the men alone.

Now food and water had been stored, clothing and blankets were ready against the cold, and certain important ceremonies to please the gods were completed. The Cliff Dwellers were prepared for the winter.

THE CLIFF DWELLERS'
DREARY WINTER

Winters were cold in the high regions inhabited by the Cliff Dwellers. During the day families huddled around fires in the courtyard to keep warm. At night, stone slabs placed across the doorways of the rooms helped to keep out the cold, but it was difficult to be really comfortable.

Those who suffered from rheumatism and arthritis could find little relief from pain. Sickness such as colds and chest diseases were common. Herbs and other medicines were used to help in curing the sick. But the people often resorted to special religious ceremonies to drive out evil spirits from the sick person. And even then, death frequently occurred.

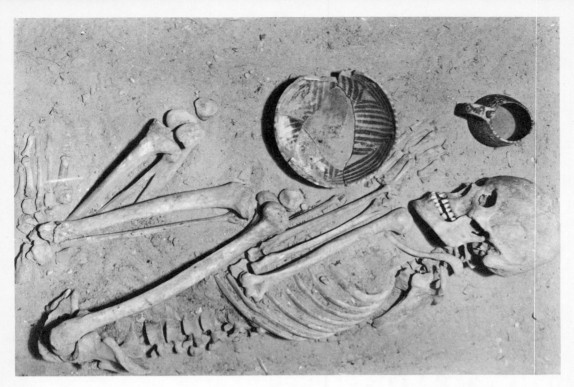

Skeleton found in a cliff dwelling shows method of burial (National Park Service)

When a person died, the body was wrapped in several layers of cloth. Nearest the body, the Cliff Dwellers usually placed a layer of feather cloth or soft cloth made of yucca fibers or cotton. Next they placed several layers of coarser cloth. A shallow grave was dug in the loose rocks at the foot of the cliff or in the trash pile outside the cave. In bad weather the grave was dug in the trash pile in the back of the cave.

The body was placed on its side with the knees drawn up toward the chin, and a bowl of food and another of water were set next to it. The shallow grave was then filled in, leav-

Metate and mano used by some Indians (Museum of American Indian, Heye Foundation)

ing hardly a trace. Some of the bodies buried in the winter in the dry trash pile in the back of the cave became mummified due to the cold and the dryness.

But winter was not only a time for discomfort, sickness, and death. It was also a time for story-telling and for singing while at work. The women were busy taking care of the babies and small children. One of their tasks was to keep a ready supply of juniper-bark diapers on hand.

Much of the women's time was spent in grinding corn and in cooking. The corn was ground in a mill made of coarse

61

rock, usually sandstone. The mill consisted of a box with a stone slab set into it at a slant. Kernels of corn were placed on the slab and rubbed against it by means of a rounded piece of rock. Some present-day Mexican Indians use a mill like it for grinding corn. They call the stone slab a *metate* and the rounded stone held in the hand a *mano*. Ethnologists use the expression "metate and mano" whenever they speak of such a mill.

The ground corn fell into the box or into a small basket placed at the bottom of the metate. The cornmeal was gritty, because grains of rock from the sandstone metate and mano rubbed off in the grinding process, and became mixed with the meal. Gritty cornmeal as a main part of their diet probably accounted for the bad teeth of so many of the Cliff Dwellers.

Cornmeal was baked into a kind of bread, or mixed with meat, beans, and other kinds of food to make soups and stews. The turkeys kept in the back of the cave supplied some of the meat.

While the women were busy with the children and with the preparation of food, the men were engaged in other work. They hunted, gathered firewood, made arrowheads, knives, and other stone implements. They sharpened long pointed digging sticks in preparation for the spring planting. For when spring came they would be so busy cultivating the fields and planting that they would have little time for tool-making.

SPRING – BUILDING, POTTERY-MAKING, AND PLANTING TIME

The busiest time of the year came in the spring. Clothing, mats, and blankets were taken out of the rooms to be aired and sunned. The floor of the cave was cleaned and swept, and the men cleaned out the kivas.

Walls were repaired and new houses built in the spring. Then there was plenty of water from melting snow to mix with plaster that had to be forced between the sandstone slabs. There was also no lack of water for moistening the colored clay used to plaster and decorate the rooms. Both men and women worked at the task of building and repair. The men did the heavy work such as lifting and placing the stones. The women helped design the rooms and applied the plaster inside and out.

63

Pottery found in cliff dwellings (National Park Service)

The children were not idle, either, for they were expected to help with the work. There was no school, but in helping the adults the children learned many skills. Thus they received training that stood them in good stead when they raised families of their own.

Because there was plenty of water at this time of the year for moistening and working clay, spring was the busiest pottery-making time. The women made the pottery. They obtained clay from beds of shale in the canyon wall or from the foot of the cliff. They ground the clay into powder and then moistened it so that it could be worked easily.

Large jars for storing water were the most important pieces of pottery made. Other pots were made mainly for cooking. The women decorated the pots with geometric designs painted on with black pigment. This was when the women could best show their creative and artistic ability, and they took special pride in their work. Then the pots were baked in a hot fire, to make them hard and waterproof. When they came from the fire the pots were a pleasing white with black designs. Some of them were truly beautiful.

But preparing the fields and planting the seeds were the two most important springtime tasks. Daily the men and older boys climbed to the top of the mesa. If necessary they cleared new land by chopping down small trees with stone axes or by burning larger trees. They used the pointed digging sticks to loosen the soil and to make it ready for seeding.

To plant corn, they dug a hole about a foot deep and dropped about ten seeds into it. Then they covered the seeds and hilled up the soil around them. Squash and beans were planted in shallower holes, perhaps no more than five seeds to a hole. For the rest of the spring, the men constantly cultivated the ground. Shifts of men and boys guarded the fields day and night to keep animals from eating first the seeds and later the tender shoots. By late spring and early summer, the plants had become sturdy and a good crop seemed assured.

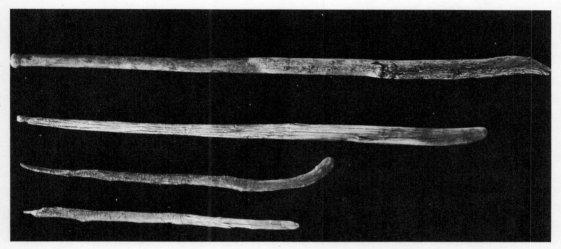

Four different kinds of digging sticks.

SUMMER, WHEN LIFE WAS EASY

Summer was the easiest time of the year for the Cliff Dwellers. Except for some cultivation of the fields and for weeding, the hard work was done. The men and boys maintained watch on the fields, but in the warm summer this was more like play than work.

By mid-summer the corn was high, but rain was scarce. To thank the gods for a good crop and to ask for rain, corn and rain festivals and dances were held. The Cliff Dwellers believed that the gods usually answered their prayers, for late summer was generally rainy. By the middle of September the ears of corn were plump and full, the beans ready to burst their pods, and the squash a ripe yellow. It was harvest time again.

HISTORY OF THE
CLIFF DWELLERS

The Cliff Dwellers began to build their dwellings about the beginning of the thirteenth century. But they must have gradually developed their method of stone and mortar building, and much of their way of life, long before that time. Archaeologists have uncovered enough evidence to give a fairly complete history of the Cliff Dwellers of Mesa Verde before the cliff houses were built. The history of other Cliff Dwellers was very much the same.

Early Basketmakers preparing for winter (Diorama in Museum at Mesa Verde National Park)

Atlatl, or spear-thrower (National Park Service)

About 2,000 years ago bands of farming Indians climbed the high cliffs and planted crops on its level top. These people have been called Basketmakers because they made very fine, closely woven baskets. They had no pottery, and no bows and arrows. Their chief weapon was the *atlatl,* a wooden spear-thrower about two feet long.

The early Basketmakers had no permanent year-round homes. They probably spent much of the year in the open fields or in simple huts made of a framework of poles covered with branches.

In winter, the Basketmakers moved into caves in the mesa cliffs. They dug small storage pits in the floor of the cave, two or three feet deep and about the same size in diameter, in which they stored food. They lined the pits with thin slabs of sandstone chinked with bark and mud. A roof of poles and packed earth, with a small open hatchway left in it, completed the pit. The hatchway could be closed by means of a thin slab of stone. If the Basketmakers left the cave for any length of time they could disguise the pits by covering them with earth.

By the year A.D. 500 important changes had taken place in the Basketmakers' way of life. This period in their history is called the period of the Modified Basketmakers. Although the people still made excellent baskets, they now had learned to make pottery as well. They had also learned to use the bow and arrow. The Basketmakers probably did not invent these new things for themselves, but borrowed the ideas from other tribes.

It is easy to imagine men who had just come from a long journey, telling of the wonderful things they had seen. One saw food cooking in a clay pot that did not burn when placed over a fire, as baskets usually do. Besides, the pot was watertight, so water could be stored in it. Another saw men shoot deer with a much more convenient weapon than the atlatl. This other weapon consisted of little "spears" shot from a bow. The little spears, really arrows, were lighter and the taut string of the bow from which they were shot sent them great distances. The travelers probably brought back with them pottery and bows and arrows to show their people.

Clay pot used especially for cooking (Mesa Verde National Park)

The Basketmakers now had permanent homes. Most of the people had moved to the top of the mesa and built pit houses, dwellings somewhat like enlarged storage pits. Some of the pit houses were as much as 20 feet in diameter. The pit itself was about three feet deep. A cone-shaped framework of poles, slightly higher than a man's head, was built around the inside of the pit. The Basketmakers covered the framework with bark, reeds, or brush, and, lastly, with a layer of earth several inches thick. As in the storage pits, an opening was left in the roof. This opening served both as a smoke hole and as an entrance.

Many of the houses had a low crawl tunnel reaching from the wall to a distance of several feet. The tunnel also helped to ventilate the pit houses. Small storage pits were dug in the floor of the main pit house. Most of the houses had a small hole, a sipapu, in the center of the floor.

The Basketmakers built pit houses and lived in them for about 250 years. But a new type of house was gradually developed. This type consisted of a number of flat-roofed, straight-walled rooms joined together in long curving rows. This type of dwelling has been called a *pueblo*, the Spanish word for village. In some places several such rows of dwellings were built parallel to each other.

The people carried on their activities in a central courtyard in front of the pueblo and on the flat roofs. Several pit houses have been found in these central courtyards. The idea for the kiva in cliff dwellings undoubtedly came from these central pit houses.

Throughout the Four Corners region, and in other parts of the Southwest, these pueblos thrived. Many of them were

Modified Basketmakers had pottery and bows and arrows. Pit houses are at the right. (Diorama in Museum at Mesa Verde National Park)

74

Pueblo of late Basketmakers built near fields on top of the mesa.
(Diorama in Museum at Mesa Verde National Park)

in river valleys, where the land was fertile. The villages became larger as more families moved into them to gain protection from bands of roving hostile Indians. But a village that was spread out was hard to defend. So the dwellings were built taller instead of spread out, to accommodate the greater population. By the middle of the eleventh century many of the pueblos consisted of terraced dwellings, some as much as four stories high. The dwellings were built of thick stone to withstand attack.

The pueblo period was generally one of peace and prosperity. But this very prosperity attracted bands of fierce marauders. It became unsafe for the people of many pueblos to live in the open fields. Those living on the mesa top therefore sought protection in the caves in the mesa cliffs, as their ancestors had done hundreds of years earlier. They brought with them the knowledge of how to build sturdy stone houses and built their many-storied terraced dwellings in the caves.

THE DISAPPEARANCE OF
THE CLIFF DWELLERS

This was the last chapter in the history of the Cliff Dwellers. They appear to have led a fairly prosperous life for about 100 years. Then the drought caused poor crops one year after another. Starvation threatened the people. Perhaps, too, they were threatened by enemy tribes even hungrier than they were. Family after family left their home in the cliff and settled in the Rio Grande valley and elsewhere in New Mexico and Arizona. Between 1275 and 1300 all of the Mesa Verde cliff dwellings were abandoned.

IN THE RIO GRANDE VALLEY

The ruins of a big settlement believed to have been inhabited by refugees from cliff dwellings can be visited today.
These ruins lie in the Frijoles Canyon of the Rio Grande valley, in Bandelier National Monument, about 45 miles from
Santa Fé, New Mexico. A creek, Rito de los Frijoles, flows
along the bottom of the canyon.

The main ruin in Bandelier National Monument is on the
canyon floor at the bottom of a cliff. The Indians call this
ruined village Tyuonyi. It consists of about 250 small rooms
built in the same style as those of the cliff dwellings. Some
of the houses are two stories tall, some appear to have been
taller.

Tyuonyi in Bandelier National Monument. Kiva is at left (National Park Service)

Most of the rock of Frijoles Canyon is volcanic tuff, a fairly soft rock. There are small natural caves in it. Many of the Cliff Dwellers who moved into the canyon enlarged the caves in the canyon wall by gouging out some of the volcanic tuff. These caves became their homes.

A number of families hacked out caves in the base of the cliff and built masonry additions at the front of the caves. These caves with their additions are called talus houses. They extend for about two miles along the cliff in Frijoles Canyon.

The people in Frijoles Canyon probably lived very much in the same way as other Cliff Dwellers. Black-on-white pottery, metates and manos, and other artifacts similar to those of Mesa Verde have been found.

Some kivas have also been found. However, the religion of the people may have changed somewhat, for a curious shrine stands about nine miles from Tyuonyi. This shrine consists of a carving of two mountain lions crouching side by side. The carving was done in an outcropping of volcanic tuff of the area. It is crudely made, but the animals are recognizable as mountain lions. No one has been able to discover for certain what these carvings mean. Scientists think the lions had some religious significance connected with hunting. In fact, some Pueblo Indian tribes still use the carvings as a hunting shrine.

← *Talus house in Bandelier National Monument (National Park Service)*

Shrine of the Stone Lions. Deer antlers between the lions were left by modern Pueblo Indians. (National Park Service)

Dwellings of modern Pueblo Indians in New Mexico (Chief of Engineers, National Archives)

Frijoles Canyon was inhabited for more than 300 years. The earliest dwelling was built at the beginning of the thirteenth century. About the time Mesa Verde and other cliff dwellings were abandoned, the population showed a marked increase. This is one reason archaeologists think refugees from other cliff dwellings moved into this region.

About the year 1550 the dwellings in Frijoles Canyon were abandoned. No one knows exactly why. All that is fairly certain is that the descendants of the people who inhabited them are among the Pueblo Indians now living in New Mexico.

A modern pueblo in the Rio Grande valley. It has glass-paned windows and a screen door. The "bee-hive" oven at the left was unknown to the Cliff Dwellers. (Bureau of Indian Affairs)

(Above)
Cliff dwellings on the Navajo Indian Reservation in Arizona (Bureau of Indian Affairs)

(Below)
Cliff dwelling on the Papago Indian Reservation. This dwelling can easily be reached by boat from a nearby lake. (Bureau of Indian Affairs)

GLOSSARY

annual ring — the growth of new wood formed each year around the trunk or branch of a tree. An annual ring is wider during a year when conditions for growth are favorable than during a year when conditions are poor.

archaeologist — a scientist who studies relics left by ancient peoples, in order to learn about their lives.

arthritis — a painful disease of the joints, such as those in the fingers and knees, which usually become inflamed and swollen.

artifact — an object made by man.

astronomer — a scientist who studies the heavens and heavenly objects.

atlatl — a wooden spear-thrower about two feet long.

Basketmakers — a group of ancient Indians, ancestors of the Cliff Dwellers, who made fine, closely woven baskets for household use.

cambium — the growth layer of a tree trunk or branch. It lies just underneath the bark. New wood is formed from the cambium.

chipping — a method of shaping a tool from stone by striking it with another stone and breaking off small pieces.

dendrochronology — a method of calculating the age of a piece of wood by counting its annual rings.

ethnologist — a scientist who studies the origin and ways of life of groups of people.

flaking — a method of forming a tool from stone by applying pressure against the part to be shaped, thus breaking off stone flakes.

Four Corners region — the area where the four states of Utah, Arizona, Colorado, and New Mexico meet.

kiva — an underground room used mainly for religious purposes by the Cliff Dwellers and by many modern Pueblo Indians.

mesa — a hill or mountain with a flat, tablelike top.

metate and mano — a mill, usually made of sandstone, used by Indians to grind corn by hand.

Mongoloid — resembling certain Asiatic groups of people who have high cheekbones, straight black hair, and eyes that appear to slant.

mummy — a dead body that has been preserved either by a drying process, or by treatment with certain chemicals.

pit house — a type of house built by ancient Indians of the Southwest. The lower part of the house was built in a big round pit dug in the ground.

plumb — a term used to describe walls which are exactly vertical with the ground.

rheumatism — a form of arthritis.

sandstone — a type of sedimentary rock formed under the sea. It is made up of grains of sand cemented together.

shale — a type of sedimentary rock formed under the sea. It is made up of clay and mud hardened into rock.

sipapu — a small hole in the center of the floor of a kiva. It is supposed to be the entrance to the underworld where the spirits of the gods live.

sunspots — dark spots that appear on the surface of the sun. Scientists think they are caused by magnetic storms on the sun.

talus house — a cave dwelling with a masonry addition at the front, such as those in the Frijoles Canyon in New Mexico.

tree-ring dating. See dendrochronology.

tree-ring profile — a diagram showing the annual rings of a log.

volcanic tuff — a fairly soft rock resulting from volcanic eruptions.

INDEX